D0604161

SACRAMENTO
KINGS

by Matt Tustison

Published by ABDO Publishing Company, 8000 West 78th Street, Edina, Minnesota 55439. Copyright © 2012 by Abdo Consulting Group, Inc. International copyrights reserved in all countries. No part of this book may be reproduced in any form without written permission from the publisher. SportsZone™ is a trademark and logo of ABDO Publishing Company.

Printed in the United States of America,
North Mankato, Minnesota
062011
092011

 THIS BOOK CONTAINS AT LEAST 10% RECYCLED MATERIALS.

Editor: Chrös McDougall
Copy Editor: Anna Comstock
Series design: Christa Schneider
Cover production: Kazuko Collins
Interior production: Carol Castro

Photo Credits: Rich Pedroncelli/AP Images, cover, 47; Neil Leifer/NBAE/Getty Images, 1; Jim Weber/AP Images, 4; Darron Cummings/AP Images, 7; Kevork Djansezian/AP Images, 9, 43 (middle); Mark J. Terrill/AP Images, 10; AP Images, 12, 42 (top), 15, 18, 42 (middle), 21, 22, 42 (bottom), 25, 29; NBAPhotos/NBAE/Getty Images, 16; Brian Horton/AP Images, 26; Dick Raphael/NBAE/Getty Images, 30, 33; Gary Stewart/AP Images, 34, 43 (top); Douglas C. Pizac/AP Images, 37; Donna McWilliam/AP Images, 39; Steve Yeater/AP Images, 41, 43 (bottom); Andy King/AP Images, 44

Library of Congress Cataloging-in-Publication Data
Tustison, Matt, 1978-
 Sacramento Kings / by Matt Tustison.
    p. cm. -- (Inside the NBA)
 Includes index.
 ISBN 978-1-61783-174-4
 1. Sacramento Kings (Basketball team)--History--Juvenile literature. I. Title.
GV885.52.S24T87 2011
 796.323'640979454--dc22
                            2011014744

TABLE OF CONTENTS

CHAPTER 1

ALMOST KINGS OF THE NBA

In 1951, the Rochester Royals basketball team won the National Basketball Association (NBA) title. Over the next several years, the team moved three times, changed its nickname from the Royals to the Kings, and ended up in Sacramento, California. Yet going into the 2001–02 season, it still had not won another title.

Simply put, the Kings franchise had not been very successful over the years. But that began to change in a big way during the mid-1990s and early 2000s. It began in 1994, when the Kings hired former NBA guard Geoff Petrie as president of basketball operations. That meant he decided who would coach and play for the team.

Another important change came at the ownership level. The Maloof family, led by brothers Joe and Gavin, bought majority ownership of the club

Kings forward Chris Webber averaged 24.5 points and 10.1 rebounds per game in 2001–02. He was named to the All-NBA Second Team.

in 1999. With the Maloofs' support, the Kings turned into a well-operated team.

The core of the Kings' 2001–02 team began to form before the 1998–99 season, when they traded for forward Chris Webber and drafted point guard Jason Williams. Petrie also signed centers Vlade Divac and Scot Pollard and hired Rick Adelman as coach. In addition, sharpshooting forward Peja Stojakovic finally joined the Kings—the team had drafted Stojakovic in 1996 and waited while the Serbian improved his game in Europe.

"We look a lot different from last year," Adelman said of the changes, "but I couldn't be happier with the core guys."

After finishing 27–55 in 1997–98, the Kings went 27–23 in the shortened 1998–99 season. That was good enough to earn a playoff berth. The Kings showed some grit in the first round of the playoffs against the heavily favored Utah Jazz. And although they were eliminated, the Kings took the series to a deciding fifth game. For his efforts in turning around the team, Petrie was named NBA Executive of the Year.

The Kings improved to 44–38 in 1999–2000. They

Kings teammates Vlade Divac, *left*, and Peja Stojakovic led their native Yugoslavia to the 2002 World Basketball Championships title.

again nearly pulled off a first-round playoff upset. In a preview of fierce battles to come, the Kings forced the Los Angeles Lakers to a fifth game before losing.

That off-season, Petrie drafted forward Hedo Turkoglu, traded for guard Doug Christie, and signed backup guard Bobby Jackson. The Kings improved to 55–27 and beat the Phoenix Suns in the first round of the playoffs. That set up another series against the Lakers in the second round. Los Angeles, led by stars Shaquille O'Neal and Kobe Bryant, swept the Kings on their way to a second straight NBA title.

With the Lakers dominating the Western Conference, Petrie knew he would have to improve the Kings' roster even further. So that off-season, he traded Williams for young point guard Mike Bibby. Williams was a crowd-pleasing dribbler and passer. But Bibby was a steady floor leader.

With Bibby's help, the 2001–02 Kings were a force. The high-scoring Kings rolled to an NBA-best 61–21 record during the regular season. In the playoffs, they cruised past Utah and the Dallas Mavericks. That set up the Western Conference finals against the Lakers.

The series was a classic. Many considered the Kings and the Lakers to be the two best teams in the NBA. And because the Lakers had eliminated the Kings in the previous two postseasons, the games quickly became heated. The teams split the first two games in Sacramento. The Kings then took the first of two in Los Angeles.

The Kings put themselves in position to take a 3–1 series lead in Game 4 when they built a 24-point lead in the first half. But then the Lakers rallied. By the final seconds of the game, Los Angeles was only down by two points and had the ball. Bryant drove and missed a shot. O'Neal grabbed the rebound

Kings point guard Mike Bibby goes up for a layup during a second-round game in the 2002 NBA Playoffs.

but could not hit on an attempt. On the rebound, Kings center Divac tried to knock the ball to a teammate. But it instead went to Lakers forward Robert Horry, who was standing outside the three-point arc. He drained a three-pointer as time expired, giving Los Angeles an unlikely 100–99 victory. NBA.com later listed the shot as one of the "Greatest Shots of the Playoffs."

The Kings bounced back in Game 5. Bibby's jump shot with 8.2 seconds left gave host Sacramento a 92–91 win at a wild ARCO Arena.

The Kings' Chris Webber drives for a layup during Game 4 of the 2002 Western Conference finals. Sacramento lost in seven games.

The Kings had a chance to win the series in Game 6 at Los Angeles. But they were hampered by foul trouble. Both Divac and Pollard fouled out. Meanwhile, O'Neal scored 41 points and made 13 of 17 free-throw tries. Los Angeles won 106–102. The Kings were called for many fouls, especially late in the contest. *Washington Post* columnist Michael Wilbon wrote, "I have never seen offici-ating in a game of consequence as bad as that in Game 6."

The series moved back to Sacramento for Game 7. It was just as close as the previous six games. Bibby made two free throws that tied the score at

100–100 and sent the game to overtime. But no Kings player besides Bibby seemed willing to take shots in the pressure-packed extra period. The Lakers pulled away and won 112–106, ending the Kings' dream season.

"They accomplished what they wanted to do. That's all I'll say about them," Webber said of the Lakers. Los Angeles went on to sweep the New Jersey Nets in the NBA Finals for the team's third consecutive title. Many basketball followers strongly believed that the Kings also would have defeated the Nets with little trouble.

Alas, the Kings never had a chance. The 2001–02 season became another one in which the Kings' franchise fell short of its ultimate goal.

PLAYOFF CONTROVERSY

The Kings' 106–102 loss to the host Lakers in Game 6 of the 2002 Western Conference finals became one of the most controversial contests in NBA history. The Lakers shot 40 free throws—27 of them in the fourth quarter alone.

Tim Donaghy was an NBA referee from 1994 to 2007. In 2007, he pleaded guilty to charges that he illegally bet on NBA games. He admitted that he gave information to gamblers, some of it regarding games he officiated, and served 13 months in prison.

Donaghy did not work Game 6, but he later claimed the NBA had instructed the officials who did to call those fouls, because the league would make more money if the series went to seven games. In 2008, NBA commissioner David Stern strongly denied the allegations, saying they were the extreme act of a convicted felon.

CHAPTER 2

BEGINNINGS IN ROCHESTER

The Kings franchise began as a semi-professional team called the Rochester Seagrams, which formed in the early 1920s in Rochester, New York. The team was sponsored by a local alcoholic beverage distillery owned by the Seagram Company.

The Seagrams played from the 1920s to the 1940s. Les Harrison helped organize the squad in its early days. The Rochester native would also play for the team and serve as its coach. He would later be enshrined in the Naismith Memorial Basketball Hall of Fame.

The semi-pro Seagrams became known as the Pros in 1943. The National Basketball League (NBL) then invited the Pros to join for the 1945–46 season. So Harrison's club became an NBL member. It also changed its name to the Rochester Royals. Harrison was the

Guard Bobby Wanzer played for the Rochester Royals from 1948 to 1957. He was one of three future Hall of Famers on the 1951 championship team, along with Bob Davies and Arnie Risen.

Royals' co-owner, coach, and general manager. His brother, Jack, was the co-owner and business manager for the team.

Rochester was an instant success in the NBL, winning the 1946 title. Guards Al Cervi and Bob Davies were two of Rochester's star players. The following season, the Royals finished 31–13. William "Dolly" King was a center/forward for the team. He became one of the first African-American players in organized basketball.

The NBL decided that the league's title would be decided during the regular season. So the Royals, with the best record, were the champions again even though they lost to the Chicago American Gears in a postseason tournament. The NBL did away with that system the next season, though. The Royals fell to the Minneapolis Lakers in the finals.

Talented Trio

Guards Bob Davies (15.2 points per game) and Bobby Wanzer (10.8), and center Arnie Risen (16.3) combined to average 42.3 points per game for the 1950–51 Royals. They were three of the key players for Rochester during that championship season. All three would eventually make the Basketball Hall of Fame. During their seven seasons together in Rochester, from 1948 to 1955, the Royals won one NBA title, qualified for the playoffs seven times, and had a winning record on six occasions.

After the 1947–48 NBL season, Harrison helped lead the way for a merger between the NBL and the Basketball Association of America (BAA). The BAA was considered the major basketball league in the United States. So Harrison's Royals and three other NBL teams moved over to the BAA for the 1948–49 season. Led by center Arnie Risen, the Royals finished first in their division.

The Royals, *in white*, guard against the New York Knickerbockers in a 1951 game. The Royals are Bob Wanzer (09), Arne Johnson (12), and Ed Mikan (18).

However, they lost to the Lakers in the division finals.

The merger between the NBL and the BAA was complete before the 1949–50 season, creating the NBA. Rochester finished tied with Minneapolis atop the Central Division with a 51–17 record. However, the Royals fell to the Fort Wayne Pistons in the playoffs.

A trio of future Hall of Fame players—Risen, Davies, and guard Bobby Wanzer—helped lead the way as Rochester compiled a 41–27 record in 1950–51. That was good for second place in their division.

The Royals started playing their best basketball at the right time in the 1951 playoffs. They topped the Pistons in the

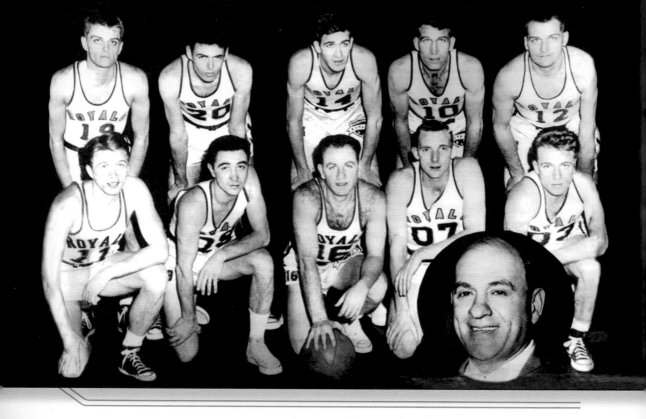

The 1951 Rochester Royals won the franchise's only NBA championship as of 2011. Among the key players were Bob Davies (11), Bobby Wanzer (09), and Arnie Risen (14).

first round and then ousted the powerful Lakers in the division finals. Rochester then played the New York Knicks in its first NBA Finals appearance.

The 1951 championship series was a classic. The Royals appeared to be on their way to an easy series victory when they won the first three games. "That Was Neat! Now Let's Go for the Sweep!" read a headline in the *Democrat and Chronicle*, Rochester's daily newspaper. However, the Knicks came back and won the next three games.

This forced a seventh and deciding game at Rochester's Edgerton Park Sports Arena. The Royals appeared to have the win locked up when they jumped out to an early 14-point lead. But New York trimmed that lead down to six by halftime. The Knicks then came out strong in the second half.

The teams traded the lead in the last two minutes. With 59 seconds left, the score was tied 75–75. The Royals took the lead when Davies made two free throws. Then forward Jack Coleman made a late basket. The 79–75 score held and the team won its only NBA championship through 2010–11. Risen led Rochester in Game 7 with 24 points and 13 rebounds. For the series, he averaged 21.7 points and 14.3 rebounds per game.

Rochester remained a top team through the mid-1950s.

Risen, Davies, and Wanzer still led the way. But the Royals could not reach the championship round. Harrison stepped down as coach after the 1954–55 season. Wanzer, who was still playing for the team, became the next coach. Davies retired, and Rochester traded Risen.

The 1955–56 Royals featured three rookies in their lineup. Forward Maurice Stokes averaged 16.8 points and 16.3 rebounds per game and was named NBA Rookie of the Year. But the Royals slipped to 31–41 and missed the NBA playoffs for the first time.

The Royals had moved into the larger Rochester Community War Memorial arena in 1955. But the club was struggling financially. After another 31–41 season in 1956–57, the Royals moved to Cincinnati, Ohio. Several of the team's players had ties to that area.

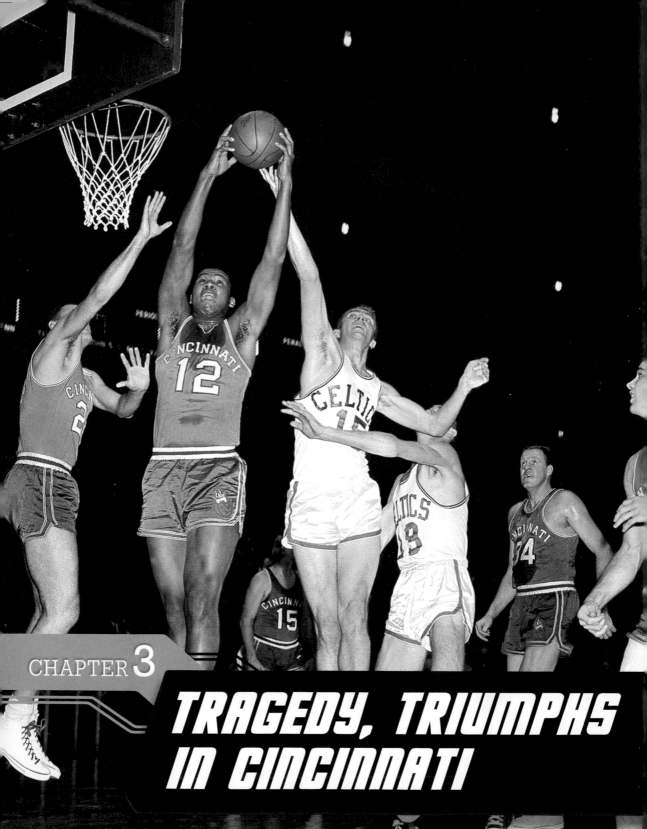

TRAGEDY, TRIUMPHS IN CINCINNATI

The Royals' move from Rochester to Cincinnati before the 1957–58 season brought some excitement to the team that had been missing in the previous few years.

The Royals acquired standout center Clyde Lovellette from the Minneapolis Lakers. He teamed with forwards Jack Twyman and Maurice Stokes to give the club a talented front-court. The Royals improved to 33–39 and returned to the playoffs.

However, a tragic injury took a toll on the team. The 6-foot-7 Stokes was among the NBA's top rebounders. But he was bumped while driving the lane in the final game of the regular season. His head slammed into the floor, and he was knocked out. Stokes eventually regained consciousness and returned to the game.

Stokes also played in Cincinnati's first playoff game. But after the team's 100–83 road loss to the Detroit Pistons in Game 1,

Cincinnati's Maurice Stokes (12) grabs a rebound during a 1958 game. He was a key player for the Royals following the move from Rochester.

Helping a Teammate

When Maurice Stokes suffered a tragic brain injury in March 1958 that eventually left him paralyzed and unable to speak, fellow Royals forward Jack Twyman aided his friend and teammate. Twyman arranged for benefit basketball games and golf tournaments that raised funds for Stokes's medical costs. Twyman also provided moral support for Stokes and his family, and he even became Stokes's legal guardian until Stokes's death in 1970. In 1973, the semi-biographical film Maurie, *starring Bernie Casey as Stokes and Bo Svenson as Twyman, portrayed the relationship between the players. The film was also known as* Big Mo.

he became ill on the Royals' flight back to Cincinnati. He was taken to the hospital when the plane landed. As the Pistons completed a sweep with a 124–104 win in Game 2, Stokes fell into a coma after suffering a seizure. He returned to consciousness in a few weeks, but he was permanently paralyzed and unable to speak.

Tests determined that Stokes had suffered a traumatic brain injury. He died of a heart attack at age 36 in 1970. Stokes was enshrined in the Basketball Hall of Fame in 2004.

Losing Stokes shook the Royals. The team sank to an NBA-worst 19–53 record in the 1958–59 season. By then, the Harrisons had sold the club to a local Cincinnati group. Although Twyman finished second in the league behind Wilt Chamberlain with 31.2 points per game in 1959–60, the Royals continued to struggle.

During that off-season, the Royals selected local star Oscar Robertson with the first pick in the NBA Draft. Robertson, a 6-foot-5 guard, had starred for the University of Cincinnati. He featured great all-around scoring, rebounding, and passing abilities. His skills showed, as he was the 1960–61 NBA

Maurice Stokes, *left*, and Jack Twyman are shown in Stokes's hospital room with their trophies as the "Most Courageous Athletes" as awarded by the Philadelphia Sports Writers Association in 1962.

Rookie of the Year. He averaged 30.5 points, 10.1 rebounds, and a league-high 9.7 assists per game. But the Royals still missed out on the playoffs.

Robertson continued to dominate during his second season. He averaged 30.8 points, 12.5 rebounds, and a league-leading 11.4 assists per contest. That meant he averaged a triple-double. Through the 2010–11 season, no other player has done that. Robertson's efforts lifted the Royals to a 43–37 record and a playoff berth. But Cincinnati fell to the Pistons in the first round.

The Royals' Oscar Robertson goes up for a shot during a 1970 game against the Chicago Bulls. He starred for the Royals from 1960 to 1970.

The Royals moved from the Western Division to the Eastern Division before the 1962–63 season. The East was home to the mighty Boston Celtics.

With Robertson leading the way, the Royals made playoff appearances each year through 1967. But Boston often spoiled things for Cincinnati. The Celtics ousted the Royals from the playoffs in 1963, 1964, and 1966. The Philadelphia 76ers also had the Royals' number. They knocked them out in the 1965 and 1967 playoffs.

Perhaps the Royals' best chance was in 1963–64. After falling to Boston in seven games in the 1963 conference finals, the Royals added star center/forward Jerry Lucas in the draft. He averaged 17.7 points and 17.4 rebounds per game and was named the NBA's Rookie of the Year. His teammate, Robertson, was chosen as the NBA's Most Valuable Player after averaging 31.4 points, 11 assists, and 9.9 rebounds per game. Behind Lucas and Robertson, the Royals finished 55–25.

Five Royals players averaged more than 10 points per game that season. They were Robertson (31.4), Lucas (17.7), center/forward Wayne Embry (17.3), Twyman (15.9), and forward Bob Boozer (11). But the Celtics eliminated the Royals in a conference finals rematch in five games. The

"THE BIG O"

Oscar Robertson, nicknamed "The Big O," was one of the best all-around players in NBA history. The 6-foot-5 guard could do it all, and his numbers back that up. After starring at the University of Cincinnati, Robertson began a Hall of Fame career with the city's NBA team in 1960.

Robertson led the NBA in assists seven times with the Royals. He also was the NBA scoring champion for the 1967–68 season, averaging 29.2 points per game. Robertson was traded to the Milwaukee Bucks after the 1969–70 season. Over his 10 seasons with the Royals, Robertson averaged a remarkable 29.3 points, 10.3 assists, and 8.5 rebounds per game.

Knicks guard Dick Barnett once said of Robertson: "If you give him a 12-foot shot, he'll work on you until he's got a 10-foot shot. Give him six, he wants four. Give him two feet and you know what he wants? That's right, man, a layup."

An Ohio Legend

Cincinnati sports fans were already familiar with Jerry Lucas before he joined the Royals in 1963. The 6-foot-8 forward had starred at Ohio State University. After his college career was over, Lucas signed with the Cleveland Pipers of the American Basketball League. But then the league folded, forcing Lucas to sit out the 1962–63 basketball season. The next year he signed with the Royals and went on to have a Hall of Fame career in the NBA. Lucas averaged more than 17 points and 17 rebounds per game in all six full seasons he played with Cincinnati. He was enshrined in the Basketball Hall of Fame in 1980.

struggling financially, also began playing many of their home games away from the Cincinnati Gardens. Contests were held in other cities such as Cleveland, Ohio. That did little to help their struggling attendance figures, though.

After two average seasons in which the Royals missed the postseason, the team fired Junker. Former Celtics star Bob Cousy replaced him as coach. The team also traded away Lucas. The result was a 36–46 finish in 1969–70. After the season, the Royals continued their makeover with the biggest move imaginable: trading Robertson.

Cincinnati sent "The Big O" to the Milwaukee Bucks in April 1970. Without Robertson and Lucas, the Royals were officially rebuilding. Cousy's teams played at a fast pace and scored plenty of points. But they gave

Celtics would go on to win the NBA crown—one of 11 league titles they won during a 13-season stretch.

The Royals began to undergo some changes during the mid-1960s. In 1966, Twyman retired and Embry was traded to Boston. In 1967, Ed Junker replaced Jack McMahon as coach. And the Royals,

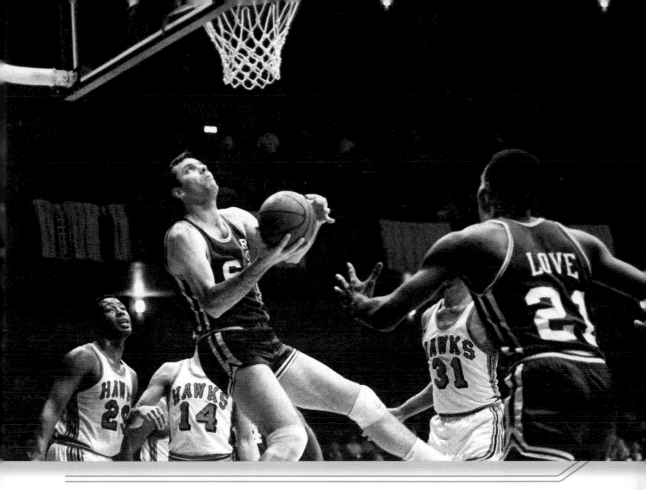

Royals big man Jerry Lucas goes up for a basket during a 1968 game against the St. Louis Hawks. He played in Cincinnati from 1963 to 1969.

up plenty as well. The Royals finished 33–49 in 1970–71.

Second-year guard Nate "Tiny" Archibald was a nice surprise for Cincinnati in the 1971–72 season. He averaged 28.2 points and 9.2 assists. But the Royals finished a mere 30–52.

That ended up being the team's last season in Cincinnati. Before the season, a group of businessmen in Kansas City, Missouri, had purchased the Royals and announced that the team would relocate for the 1972–73 campaign.

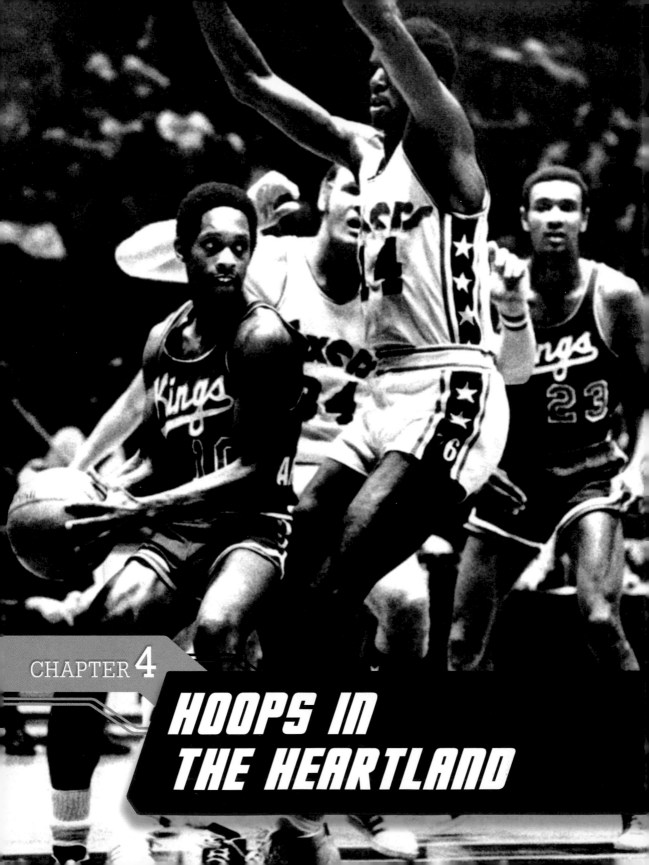

CHAPTER 4

HOOPS IN THE HEARTLAND

Coincidentally, the Major League Baseball team in Kansas City was also named the Royals. So when the basketball team moved there for the 1972–73 season, it changed its name to the Kings. And since the team played many of its home games in Omaha, Nebraska, it officially became known as the Kansas City-Omaha Kings.

The Kings' first season in America's heartland was a good one for guard Nate "Tiny" Archibald. Archibald led the NBA in scoring (34 points per game) and assists (11.4 per game). That made him the first player in league history to rank first in both of those categories in the same season. However, Archibald did not receive much help. As a result, the Kings finished only 36–46 and did not reach the postseason.

The 1973–74 season was not any better. Archibald played

Kansas City Kings star Nate Archibald dribbles around Philadelphia 76ers defender Leroy Ellis during a 1972 game.

A "TINY" STAR

Nate "Tiny" Archibald was one of the top players in Kings history and the franchise's best player when it was based in Kansas City. However, the 6-foot-1, 150-pound guard received the nickname "Tiny" after his father, who was called "Big Tiny." When Archibald's father left his family, Nate, only 14 years old at the time, took on more responsibility at home. And he did so while avoiding the temptations of the street.

"It's interesting," Archibald once said, "how guys who are into drugs are always looking to get other guys involved, as if they want company when they go under. Me? I was always into basketball."

Archibald was a speedy and creative playmaker who was equally skilled at scoring and sharing the ball with teammates. Later in his career, Archibald helped the Boston Celtics win the 1981 league title. He was enshrined in the Basketball Hall of Fame in 1991.

in only 35 games because of an ankle injury. Coach Bob Cousy was fired after the Kings started 6–16. The team played better under eventual replacement Phil Johnson. But the Kings still finished only 33–49 and again missed the playoffs.

With Archibald healthy again and center Sam Lacey becoming an inside force, the Kings improved to 44–38 in 1974–75. That earned the club its first playoff berth since 1967. Johnson was named the league's Coach of the Year. However, the Kings lost in the first round of the playoffs.

The Kings dropped the Omaha portion of their name for the 1975–76 season, even though they still played some games in Omaha. After a disappointing 31–51 season, the Kings traded Archibald to the New York Nets. In return they got guard Brian Taylor, center

The Kings' Otis Birdsong escapes with the ball after stealing it from the Detroit Pistons' Bob Lanier during a 1979 game in Kansas City.

Jim Eakins, and two first-round draft picks.

The Kings improved to 40–42 in 1976–77. However, a poor finish kept them out of the postseason. They fell to a 31–51 record in 1977–78, and Johnson was fired as coach partway through the season.

The Kings took a big step forward in 1978–79. The club hired veteran NBA coach Cotton Fitzsimmons. Meanwhile, the draft picks obtained in the Archibald trade resulted in guards Otis Birdsong and Phil Ford, who both quickly developed into key players.

Kings swingman Scott Wedman looks to make a play during a 1980 game. He played for the Kings from 1974 to 1981.

Birdsong scored 21.7 points per game. Ford was good for 15.9 points and 8.6 assists per game, earning him the NBA's Rookie of the Year Award. Fitzsimmons was selected as the NBA's Coach of the Year, as well. And the Kings, who no longer played any home games in Omaha, finished 48–34 and won the Midwest Division title.

The Kings' positive season ended with frustration in the postseason, though. After receiving a first-round bye, they fell to the Phoenix Suns four games to one in the second round.

The Kings came right back in 1979–80 with another strong season. Birdsong and Ford again led the way, and Kansas City finished 47–35. The Kings again faced the Suns in the playoffs. But Phoenix prevailed once more, ousting Kansas City two games to one in the first-round matchup.

Birdsong averaged 24.6 points per game in 1980–81. Scott Wedman, Ford, and second-year forward Reggie King also played well. The Kings finished a mediocre 40–42. But they played much better in the playoffs by implementing a new strategy. They began using 6-foot-6 Ernie Grunfeld at the point guard spot and played a slower-paced game. Kansas City beat the Portland Trail Blazers two games to one in the first round, marking the club's first postseason series victory since 1964.

And the Kings did not stop there. They met the Suns for a third straight year in the playoffs. They finally topped Phoenix, winning 95–88 in Game 7 on the road to take the series.

This put Kansas City in the Western Conference finals against the Houston Rockets. Like the Kings, the Rockets had finished the regular season 40–42. However, led by star center Moses Malone, Houston proved to be the stronger team. The Rockets won four games to one.

The hope was that the Kings could build on their playoff success. However, the team's roster looked much different when the next season began. The Cleveland Cavaliers signed Wedman to a big free-agent contract. And the Kings dealt Birdsong and a second-round draft pick to the

Nets for forward Cliff Robinson. Robinson averaged 20.2 points and 8.5 rebounds per game with Kansas City in 1981–82. But he was traded to Cleveland in midseason for forward/center Reggie Johnson. The Kings struggled to a 30–52 record.

Point guard Larry Drew and sharpshooting forward

Eddie Johnson led the Kings to a 45–37 record in 1982–83. But in a competitive Western Conference, that mark was not good enough for a playoff berth. Kansas City slipped to 38–44 in 1983–84. But this time, the record earned the Kings a post-season spot. However, Kansas City fell three games to none to the Los Angeles Lakers in the first round.

Before the 1983–84 season, the Kings were sold to a group of investors from Sacramento, California. Then, after the 1983–84 season, Fitzsimmons stepped down to coach the San Antonio Spurs, leaving former Lakers and Indiana Pacers coach Jack McKinney to replace him.

An all-too-familiar situation was brewing, though. Kansas City started terribly in 1984–85. McKinney resigned and was replaced by Johnson,

Attendance Woes

During the Kings' 13 seasons in Kansas City, the team never ranked in the top half of the NBA in attendance and was among the bottom five teams six times. Attendance reached a low point after the club's owners announced during the 1984–85 campaign that the Kings would relocate to Sacramento the next season. The average attendance for Kings home games in 1984–85 was just 6,410 fans per game, and the team ranked last out of 23 NBA clubs. On April 14, 1985, a larger than usual crowd of 11,371 turned out at Kemper Arena to see the Kings play their last game in Kansas City—a 122–116 loss to the Los Angeles Lakers.

The Kings' Larry Drew faces off against Boston Celtics defender Quinn Buckner during a 1984 game.

who had previously coached the Kings from 1973 to 1978. As the team continued to struggle, the owners announced that the Kings would relocate to Sacramento the following season. The Kings finished 31–51 and in last place. Shortly thereafter, the club was moving yet again.

CHAPTER 5

THE SACRAMENTO YEARS

The move to Sacramento before the 1985–86 season was the Kings' third. The Atlanta Hawks are the only other NBA team to have moved three times. Sacramento appeared to be a good fit, though. The Kings were the city's first professional sports team, and fans strongly supported them, which was a relief for the owners of the struggling team.

The Kings actually reached the playoffs in their first season in California, finishing 37–45. However, the Houston Rockets swept them in the first round. It would be the Kings' last time in the postseason for 10 years.

Poor draft selections and tragedies off the court were factors as the Kings failed to win more than 29 games in a season from 1986–87 through 1993–94. The team changed coaches often, but it was to no avail.

Kings forward Ricky Berry dunks the ball over Seattle SuperSonics defenders during a 1989 game.

Supportive Fans

From 1985 to 1988, the Kings played at the original ARCO Arena. That arena seated only about 10,000 fans, and every Kings game held there sold out. The team moved into a new ARCO Arena, sometimes called ARCO Arena II, in 1988. That arena seated more than 17,000, and even though the Kings were not successful, fans continued to support them. The club's sellout streak continued for years, finally ending at 497 games on November 7, 1997, in a 98–85 loss to the Los Angeles Clippers. Through the 2010–11 NBA season, this was the fourth-longest home sellout streak in league history. The Kings then went on another long stretch of games with capacity crowds. From November 1999 to November 2007, the team sold out 354 contests in a row. This ranked as the fifth-longest streak in NBA history through 2010–11.

The Kings had some talented players during their early years in Sacramento. Guard Reggie Theus, forwards Wayman Tisdale and Lionel Simmons, and especially guard Mitch Richmond were among

them. Richmond led the Kings in scoring in each of his seven seasons with the team, from 1991–92 to 1997–98. But the club did not have enough quality players at any one time to build a strong squad.

The team's fortunes began to change when it hired Geoff Petrie as president of basketball operations in 1994. But it would take some time.

The Kings suffered through their 13th straight losing season in 1995–96. However, their 39–43 record was good enough to get them into the playoffs for the first time since 1986. Sacramento, led by Richmond and forwards Walt "The Wizard" Williams and Brian Grant, could not overcome the mighty Seattle SuperSonics, though. Seattle swept the Kings in three games.

Sacramento's struggles continued as the team suffered

Kings forward Chris Webber drives against John Stockton of the Utah Jazz during a 1999 game.

through two more losing seasons. The Kings missed the playoffs both times.

The turning point occurred before the 1998–99 season, when the Kings traded for forward Chris Webber, signed center Vlade Divac, and hired veteran NBA coach Rick Adelman. With a 27–23 record in the shortened season and a playoff berth, the Kings' era of excellence had begun. Now owned by the Maloof family, led by brothers Joe and Gavin, the club would make the playoffs for eight consecutive seasons.

Petrie would add more key players. Kings players such as Webber, Divac, point guard

TRAGEDY

Part of the reason the Kings struggled during their first decade in Sacramento was that several players who were high draft picks did not develop into quality, long-term players for the team. In some cases, this was because of off-the-court tragedies.

In 1988, the Kings drafted forward Ricky Berry in the first round. Berry had a strong rookie season for Sacramento, averaging 11 points per game in 1988–89. Sadly, Berry committed suicide after the season.

Four years later, the Kings selected point guard Bobby Hurley in the NBA Draft's first round. In December 1993, Hurley was driving home after a game at ARCO Arena when he was involved in a car accident and suffered life-threatening injuries. He rejoined the Kings for the 1994–95 season and played with the team until 1998. But he never developed into a top NBA player.

Mike Bibby, guards Doug Christie and Bobby Jackson, forwards Peja Stojakovic and Hedo Turkoglu, and center Scot Pollard gave the Kings a balanced and deep roster. Many fans enjoyed watching the Kings play for their passing abilities and exciting offensive style.

However, the team always fell just short in the playoffs. The closest they got to reaching the NBA Finals was in 2001–02, when they lost to the Los Angeles Lakers in the conference finals. After that, the Kings lost to the Dallas Mavericks and the Minnesota Timberwolves in the second rounds of the next two seasons, respectively.

The Kings' window of opportunity was closing. They had traded Pollard and Turkoglu for star center Brad

From left, Mike Bibby, Vlade Divac, and Peja Stojakovic watch as the Kings lose to the Dallas Mavericks during a 2004 playoff game.

Miller before the 2003–04 season. Divac signed with the Lakers before the next season. Then, during the 2004–05 season, the Kings traded ace defensive player Christie, and later Webber. With their new core of players, the Kings finished the season 50–32, but fell to the Sonics in the first round of the playoffs.

The moves continued. The Kings sent Stojakovic to the Indiana Pacers for forward Ron Artest during the 2005–06 season. But Sacramento slipped to 44–38 and fell in the postseason's first round. The Kings fired Adelman after the season. He left with 395 regular-season wins—the most in club history.

New Sacramento coach Eric Musselman lasted just one season, finishing 33–49 in 2006–07. One bright spot was the emergence of guard Kevin Martin, who scored 20.2 points per game. Theus, now retired as a player, became the Kings' coach in 2007–08. The team finished 38–44. In February of that season, Sacramento sent Bibby to the Atlanta Hawks.

The Kings were clearly in a rebuilding mode. They traded Artest, one of the league's best defensive players, before the 2008–09 season. Theus was dismissed as coach shortly into that campaign and replaced by Kenny Natt. Sacramento limped to a 17–65 record—the worst in the NBA.

That would prove to be the low point for the Kings. They brought in veteran NBA coach Paul Westphal for the 2009–10 season. They also traded high-scoring Martin and forward Hilton Armstrong for young forwards Joey Dorsey and Carl Landry. Meanwhile, draft pick Tyreke Evans quickly became a star. Evans, a 6-foot-6 guard, averaged 20.1 points, 5.8 assists, and 5.3 rebounds per game. He was the NBA's Rookie of the Year even though the Kings finished just 25–57.

The Kings added power forward DeMarcus Cousins with the fifth pick in the 2010 NBA

Tyreke Evans had a stellar rookie season in 2009–10, when he averaged 20.1 points, 5.8 assists, and 1.5 steals per game.

Draft. He was a strong scorer and rebounder for Sacramento during the 2010–11 season. However, the Kings again failed to reach the playoffs.

With a young core of players including Evans and Cousins, the Kings have a bright future.

Whether that future is in Sacramento, however, is unknown. As the fan base has dwindled and the Kings' arena has continued to get older, the owners have considered once again moving the team.

TIMELINE

1946
Playing their first season in the professional NBL, the Rochester Royals, coached by Les Harrison, sweep the Sheboygan Red Skins in three games in the finals to capture the title.

1951
In their second season in the NBA—which was created as the result of a merger between the BAA and the NBL—the Royals capture the league's title. Rochester wins four games to three over the New York Knicks in the NBA Finals. Arnie Risen's 24 points and 13 rebounds lift the host Royals to a 79–75 victory in Game 7 on April 21.

1958
The Royals play their first season based in Cincinnati, and it ends tragically when All-Star forward Maurice Stokes is knocked unconscious after a fall on March 12 against host Minneapolis. Stokes suffered a brain injury that days later would result in a seizure and leave him permanently paralyzed and unable to speak.

1961
Royals guard Oscar Robertson is named NBA Rookie of the Year after averaging 30.5 points, 10.1 rebounds, and 9.7 assists per game.

1962
Robertson becomes the first player in NBA history to average a triple-double for a season. He scores 30.8 points per game, grabs 12.5 rebounds a contest, and hands out 11.4 assists per game.

1967
Center-forward Jerry Lucas and Robertson help lift Cincinnati to a sixth consecutive playoff berth. But for the sixth straight year, the Royals cannot reach the NBA Finals. They fall three games to one to the Philadelphia 76ers in the Eastern Division semifinals.

1973	The team, renamed the Kings, finishes its initial season based in Kansas City-Omaha. Kings guard Nate "Tiny" Archibald becomes the first player in NBA history to lead the league in scoring and assists in the same season. He averages 34 points and 11.4 assists per game.

1986	The Kings finish their first season based in Sacramento with a 37–45 record. The team falls three games to none to the Rockets in the first round of the playoffs.
1994	Former Portland Trail Blazers guard and executive Geoff Petrie is hired as the Kings' vice president of basketball operations.
1999	The Maloof family, led by brothers Joe and Gavin, purchases majority control of the Kings.

2002	With new point guard Mike Bibby helping lead the way, the Kings finish an NBA-best 61–21. Sacramento eliminates the Utah Jazz and the Dallas Mavericks in the postseason's first two rounds. The Kings then fall to the rival Los Angeles Lakers in the Western Conference finals. On June 2, Los Angeles beats host Sacramento 112–106 in Game 7 in overtime.
2006	The Kings finish 44–38 and then lose four games to two to the San Antonio Spurs in the first round of the postseason. It is the last of eight years in a row in which Sacramento makes the playoffs. Adelman is fired as coach after the season.

2010	After averaging 20.1 points, 5.8 assists, and 5.3 rebounds per game for the 2009–10 season, Kings guard Tyreke Evans, a former University of Memphis star, is named NBA Rookie of the Year.

QUICK STATS

FRANCHISE HISTORY

Rochester Royals (1948–57)
Cincinnati Royals (1957–72)
Kansas City-Omaha Kings (1972–75)
Kansas City Kings (1975–85)
Sacramento Kings (1985–)

NBA FINALS
(1950– ; win in bold)

1951

KEY PLAYERS
(position[s]; years with team)

Nate "Tiny" Archibald (G; 1970–76)
Mike Bibby (G; 2001–08)
Bob Davies (G/F; 1948–55)
Vlade Divac (C; 1999–2004)
Wayne Embry (C/F; 1958–66)

Tyreke Evans (G; 2009–)
Jerry Lucas (F/C; 1963–69)
Arnie Risen (C/F; 1948–55)
Oscar Robertson (G/F; 1960–70)
Peja Stojakovic (F/G; 1999–2006)
Maurice Stokes (F/C; 1955–58)
Jack Twyman (F/G; 1955–66)
Bobby Wanzer (G; 1948–57)
Chris Webber (F/C; 1998–2005)

KEY COACHES

Rick Adelman (1999–2006):
    395–229; 34–35 (postseason)
Les Harrison (1948–55):
    295–181; 19–19 (postseason)

HOME ARENAS

Edgerton Park Sports Arena
    (1948–55)
Rochester Community War Memorial
    (1955–57)
Cincinnati Gardens (1957–72)
Municipal Auditorium (1972–74,
    1978–79)
Omaha Civic Auditorium (1972–78)
Kemper Arena (1974–79, 1980–85)
ARCO Arena I (1985–88)
Power Balance Pavilion (1988–)
    Known as ARCO Arena II
    (1988–2011)

* All statistics through 2010–11 season

QUOTES AND ANECDOTES

The 1945–46 Rochester Royals, who won the NBL title in their first season in the league, had several players who would go on to become standouts outside of basketball. Otto Graham, a 6-foot-1 guard for Rochester's 1946 NBL title team, went on to have a legendary football career as a quarterback for the Cleveland Browns. Also on that Royals squad was Chuck Connors, a forward who would also play professional baseball as a first baseman with the Brooklyn Dodgers and the Chicago Cubs. The 6-foot-5 Connors would gain even more fame as an actor, most famously as the title character in the TV Western *The Rifleman*, which ran from 1958 to 1963. And Del Rice, a 6-foot-2 guard, was yet another two-sport athlete for the Royals. Baseball was his better sport—he was a major league catcher from 1945 to 1961 for five teams.

"Robertson was a big man with the moves of a really tremendous little man."
—Former Boston Celtics guard Bill Sharman, on 6-foot-5 guard Oscar Robertson, who starred for the Cincinnati Royals from 1960 to 1970

In the 1990–91 season, Sacramento had a 1–40 record in games away from home. This set an NBA record for the worst road record in an 82-game season. The Kings managed to go 24–17 in home games that season.

Wayman Tisdale was a standout forward for the Kings from 1989 to 1994. The 6-foot-9 Tisdale averaged at least 20 points per game in 1989–90 and 1990–91. Tisdale was also was a musician. He played the bass guitar and released eight jazz albums. Tisdale was diagnosed with cancer in his right leg in 2007, and part of the leg had to be amputated. He died suddenly in 2009 at the age of 44 when he was taken to the hospital after he had trouble breathing. It was not known whether his death was related to his battle with cancer.

GLOSSARY

attendance

The number of fans at a particular game or who come to watch a team play during a particular season.

berth

A place, spot, or position, such as in the NBA playoffs.

contract

A binding agreement about, for example, years of commitment by a basketball player in exchange for a given salary.

draft

A system used by professional sports leagues to select new players in order to spread incoming talent among all teams. The NBA Draft is held each June.

free agent

A player whose contract has expired and who is able to sign with a team of his choice.

general manager

The executive who is in charge of the team's overall operation. He or she hires and fires coaches, drafts players, and signs free agents.

interim

Temporary.

playoffs

A series of games in which the winners advance in a quest to win a championship.

retire

To officially end one's career.

rookie

A first-year player in the NBA.

triple-double

When a player reaches double digits in three different categories during one game, such as points, assists, rebounds, steals, or blocked shots.

veteran

An individual with great experience in a particular endeavor.

FOR MORE INFORMATION

Further Reading

Ballard, Chris. *The Art of a Beautiful Game: The Thinking Fan's Tour of the NBA*. New York: Simon & Schuster, 2009.

Reynolds, Jerry, with Don Drysdale. *Reynolds Remembers: 20 Years with the Sacramento Kings*. Champaign, IL: Sports Publishing, 2006.

Robertson, Oscar. *The Big O: My Life, My Times, My Game*. Lincoln, NE: Bison Books, 2010.

Web Links

To learn more about the Sacramento Kings, visit ABDO Publishing Company online at **www.abdopublishing.com**. Web sites about the Kings are featured on our Book Links page. These links are routinely monitored and updated to provide the most current information available.

Places to Visit

Kemper Arena & Sports Complex
1800 Genessee
Kansas City, MO 64102
816-949-7100
www.kemperarenakc.com
This was the Kings' home arena for most of their time in Kansas City in the 1970s and 1980s. These days, it hosts concerts, basketball games, and other events.

Naismith Memorial Basketball Hall of Fame
1000 West Columbus Avenue
Springfield, MA 01105
413-781-6500
www.hoophall.com
This hall of fame and museum highlights the greatest players and moments in the history of basketball. Oscar Robertson and Nate "Tiny" Archibald are among the former players from the Kings franchise who are enshrined here.

Power Balance Pavilion
1 Sports Parkway
Sacramento, CA 95834
916-455-4647
www.powerbalancepavilion.com
Formerly known as ARCO Arena II, this has been the Kings' home arena since the 1988—89 season.

INDEX

About the Author

Matt Tustison is a sports copy editor at the *Palm Beach Post* in Florida. He previously worked as an editor and writer of sports books for the educational market at Red Line Editorial in Burnsville, Minnesota. He also has been a sports copy editor at the *Baltimore Sun* and the *St. Paul Pioneer Press*, as well as a freelance sports reporter for the Associated Press in Minneapolis.